# Deadly Venom:

# Killer or Cure?

Written by Kerrie Shanahan

**Flying Start**
to Literacy®

# Contents

# Introduction

Many animals produce poison and venom, which they use to protect themselves or to kill other animals for food. Poison and venom are not only deadly and dangerous to other animals, but also to people. But now scientists believe that the venom and poison these animals produce can help people.

Scientists have investigated poison and venom from a range of animals and they have discovered some amazing ways to use it. Some venoms and poisons are used to help save lives, to stop people feeling pain, to fight diseases and to create pesticides.

## Did you Know?

Both venom and poison are toxins and they can be dangerous if they get into your body. Venom gets into your body by a bite or a sting. Poison has to be swallowed or inhaled.

# Chapter 1
# Surviving the bite

Many spiders, snakes and scorpions have venom. They inject venom into their victims by biting or stinging them. Most venom stops prey from moving so that it cannot get away and can be easily eaten.

Once the venom has been injected into the victim, it targets nerve and muscle cells. This stops messages being sent to and from muscles. It also stops the muscles from working normally

The redback spider injects venom when it bites.

The fangs of the rattlesnake release venom into its victim.

If a person is bitten or stung by an animal with venom, getting medical help is very important. If possible, the person needs to be able to describe the animal, as this helps the doctor to know how to treat the person. The doctor will then give the person something called antivenom. Antivenom stops the venom from working and saves the person's life.

# Making antivenom

Antivenom is made from the venom of that particular animal. It is made by injecting another animal such as a horse or sheep with the venom. This animal begins to make antibodies to fight the venom in its body. These antibodies are then collected and used to make the antivenom.

Antivenom works like a vaccination. When injected with antivenom, a person's body begins to make antibodies to fight the venom.

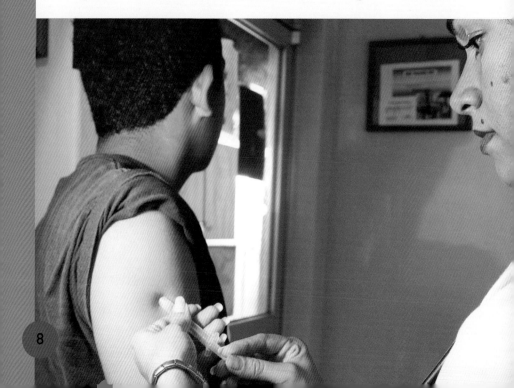

Spider venom is collected.

## Collecting venom

Scientists have to collect an animal's venom to make antivenom. This is dangerous work. Venom collectors keep these animals in tanks. They look after and feed the animals to keep them healthy.

### Did you Know?

Spider venom is collected by making a spider angry. As the venom forms in droplets on the spider's fangs, it is collected on a thin stick and dropped into a container.

# Chapter 2
# Deadly venom or lifesaver?

Many animals have venom or poison that is deadly and can kill a person in seconds. The venom or poison of these deadly animals helps them to catch prey, to digest food or to defend themselves.

Rattlesnake venom is collected.

Scientists collect poison and venom from many deadly animals. They study the way that venom and poison work and use this information to help people.

Venom and poison are now being used to make medicines and treatments that can save people's lives. In the future scientists predict that there will be many more uses for venom in medicine.

# Eastern brown snake

The eastern brown snake is one of the world's deadliest snakes. When it attacks, it raises itself up and strikes rapidly with its mouth open. It bites its victim, injecting venom. The venom makes the victim's blood form clots. When the clots form, the blood cannot move around the body and the victim can die.

Scientists have isolated the part of the venom that causes blood to form clots, and they have used it to make a life-saving spray.

The eastern brown snake lives in Australia. It has killed more people in Australia than any other snake.

Venom is collected from a snake.

When someone is badly injured, that person can lose a lot of blood very quickly. They can bleed to death in as little as four minutes. The spray made from the snake's venom helps to stop the very fast blood loss.

Scientists collect snake venom by holding the snake's head and making it bite the rubber lid of a glass container. The snake's fangs go through the rubber and the venom drips into the container.

# Death stalker scorpion

The death stalker scorpion is deadly and dangerous. It is an aggressive scorpion that has small, narrow pincers and extremely strong venom. It has a stinger on the end of its tail which it uses to inject venom into its victim. The venom attacks the nervous system of the victim. This can cause painful muscle spasms, paralysis and even death.

A scorpion catches its prey.

Scientists have discovered that one part of the scorpion's venom can kill cancer cells. They are using it to treat certain types of brain cancer. The toxin attacks only the cancer cells. The normal brain cells are not harmed.

Scientists collect scorpion venom by holding the scorpion at a safe distance using a long tool. The scorpion is then given a mild electric shock that causes it to shoot out venom. The venom is collected in a tube.

# Golden poison arrow frog

The golden poison arrow frog has poisonous
skin. There is enough poison in the skin of
one frog to kill up to ten people. If a person
or animal touches the frog, poison seeps out
of small glands on the frog's skin. The
poison can enter the victim's blood stream.
It attacks nerve cells and stops these cells from
sending messages. This affects the victim's
muscles and can cause heart failure and death.

## Did you Know?

Tribes in Central and South America used to put poison from poison arrow frogs into their arrow tips.

Scientists have discovered that a part of this poison can be used to stop pain messages being sent to the brain. This part of the frog's poison is being used to create a new pain-killing medicine.

Scientists collect poison from poison arrow frogs by stroking their skin with a metal wand that has a very small amount of electricity running through it. This makes poison ooze through the frogs' skin. The poison is then washed off and collected.

# Blue-ringed octopus

The blue-ringed octopus is one of the deadliest animals in the sea. It has very strong venom in its saliva that can kill people. The octopus uses its horny beak to bite the victim. The venom in the saliva seeps into the wound. The venom blocks all messages that travel from the nerves to the muscles, which stops the victim from moving. The victim becomes paralysed and dies.

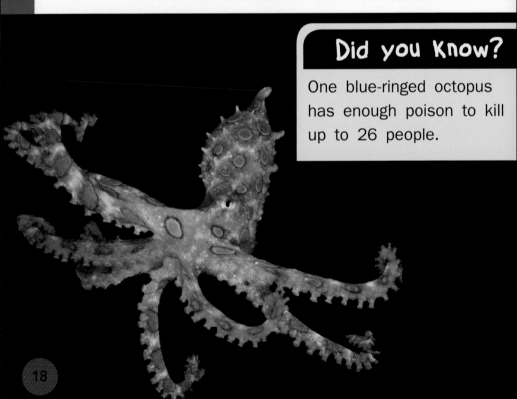

## Did you Know?

One blue-ringed octopus has enough poison to kill up to 26 people.

Scientists have discovered that a part of
the blue-ringed octopus venom also stops
pain messages being sent to the brain.
They have used this part of the venom
to make a drug that stops people from
feeling pain.

To get its venom, scientists put the octopus in
a plastic bag and make it angry. When it
bites through the bag, the venom flows out
of the hole and is collected in a plastic tube.

# Chapter 3

# Funnel-web spiders: farmers' friends?

The funnel-web spider is one of the world's deadliest spiders.  It is an aggressive spider that uses its strong fangs to inject venom into its victims.  The venom can kill a person in less than an hour.

Scientists have discovered that the funnel-web spider's venom has over 200 different parts. Each part of the venom works on different animals. One part only affects mice. Another part only affects cockroaches. Scientists are using this information to investigate the use of funnel-web spider venom in protecting crops from pests.

## Did you Know?

Dogs and cats can survive 100 times the amount of venom that can kill people.

# Killing pests

Insect pests are a massive problem for farmers all over the world. Pests destroy about one-third of the world's crops each year. Some pests such as grasshoppers and locusts destroy crops that are grown for food. Some farmers use pesticides, which are poisons, to kill the pests and save their crops.

Many pesticides kill all insects in a field including bees and other insects that help plants to grow. These pesticides also pollute the environment and can enter water systems, and make people sick if they drink the water.

Scientists have used parts of the funnel-web spider's venom to make a pesticide that only affects the insects that destroy crops. It does not kill other insects such as bees and it does not harm the environment.

A plague of locusts destroys a crop.

# Chapter 4
# Into the future

In the future we may see more breakthroughs as scientists explore different ways that the venom from deadly and dangerous animals can be used.

Scientists are working on using the saliva from ticks and the poison from some frogs to produce drugs to treat heart disease.

Jumper ants could be used to make medicine that lowers blood pressure. The venom from some types of sea snakes could be used to treat heart conditions.

The venom of blue poison arrow frogs could help in the treatment of heart disease.

A lot of these investigations are still very new, but scientists believe that they will lead to new discoveries such as cures for diseases. Venom and poison may one day save your life.

# Glossary

**antivenom**   A liquid that stops venom from working

**clot**   A thick lump of liquid

**inject**   To force liquid into the body, usually with something sharp

**isolate**   To separate something from other things

**nerve cell**   Tiny parts of the body that send messages between the brain and the nerves. Nerves control the sense of touch and pain

**nervous system**   The system of nerves in the body that carries messages to and from the brain

**paralysis**   Not being able to move or have any feeling in a part or all of the body

**spasms**   A sudden tightening of the muscles that can cause the body to twist or shake

**toxin**   Poison produced by a living thing

# A note from the author

My eight-year-old son and I loved watching a documentary series on television called *Deadly 60*. It was about the most deadly animals in the world. I thought that kids would love to read about these sorts of animals.

Once I started researching the topic, I was amazed to find out that the venom and poison from some deadly animals are actually being used to help people.

I also watched a documentary called *The Venom Cure*. It is about the different ways that scientists are using venom from poisonous animals to help people. It was exciting to learn about how animals that we generally try to avoid can be of great benefit to us.